MY
Flower
Garden
LIFE

————

CHRISTIE PURIFOY

HARVEST HOUSE PUBLISHERS
EUGENE, OREGON

Published in association with The Bindery Agency, www.TheBinderyAgency.com.

Cover and interior design by Leah Beachy
Cover and interior artwork © merfin, nastyasklyarova, ArinaKram / Adobe Stock

For bulk, special sales, or ministry purchases, please call 1-800-547-8979.
Email: CustomerService@hhpbooks.com

This logo is a federally registered trademark of the Hawkins Children's LLC. Harvest House Publishers, Inc., is the exclusive licensee of this trademark.

My Flower Garden Life

Copyright © 2024 by Christie Purifoy
Published by Harvest House Publishers
Eugene, Oregon 97408
www.harvesthousepublishers.com

ISBN 978-0-7369-8957-2 (Flexibound)

Printed in China

24 25 26 27 28 29 30 31 32 / RDS / 10 9 8 7 6 5 4 3 2 1

CONTENTS

How to Enjoy This Book

AND MAKE IT YOUR OWN

———

Tending a garden isn't like other hobbies. In fact, I hesitate to call it a hobby at all, for while it is a creative—even artistic—activity, it isn't like knitting or painting or bird-watching or bread baking. While those things fill time in wonderful ways, gardening actively shapes time. Gardening is not a pastime by which we pass the time creatively and productively. Rather, it is one of the most life-giving ways in which we *keep* time.

If time sometimes feels like an enemy, then let this be one more reason why it is good to live as a garden maker and a garden keeper: gardens are forms of beauty that unfold only in time. Like music, they turn the passage of time into a work of art. My flower garden life is exactly that—a way of life. Because I grow a garden, my life keeps a rhythm. Time is no longer an ordinary straight line but a beautiful circle, always returning yet always new. In my garden, I have not only made peace with time; I have become friends with time. After all, it is time that transforms my offering of a seed into the harvest of a beautiful bouquet.

A flower garden is much more than a list of chores. My garden isn't one more "to-do" in a life that is already overfull with commitments and obligations. Instead, gardening has shaped my days and weeks and years with a gently repeating rhythm of dreaming, preparing, sowing, tending, and gathering. My flower garden life is a life of anticipation because there is always something good to look forward to when we grow a garden.

Though time is the most critical ingredient in our garden making, this planner is not organized according to the four seasons. You will not find in these pages a list of garden tasks for each month, though there will be space for you to record meaningful dates as you observe the growth of your own flowers. Instead, I encourage you to approach this book—and indeed the whole year—like a circle you can step into at any point along the way. If you have always believed gardens must begin in spring, if summer heat or winter cold holds sway and gardening feels impossible, then may this book help you take a first step no matter the time of year. Gardens begin with dreams, and we can dream with a seed catalog on our laps whether we're resting in the air-conditioned heat of summer or enjoying a fire on a winter night.

Because garden time is circular, this book is meant to be a helpful companion and guide no matter where you are in your garden year. You might crack open *Part One: Dream* when the new seed and plant catalogs arrive in January. You might return to those pages in the high heat of late summer when your enthusiasm for gardening has flagged and you need to dream a little of cooler days and springtime flowers. *Part Two: Prepare* could be equally helpful when prepping a new garden area in the fall or if you discover in midsummer that you really do need a new spot for all the bearded irises you've multiplied through division.

In *Part Three: Sow, Plant, and Tend*, you will find my "Annual Rhythm of Garden Tasks," but even here the tasks are not date-specific (which is important not only because we garden in different growing zones but because climate and weather patterns are shifting for all of us). Instead, this annual guide gives us a picture of the whole garden year and helps us see which garden tasks belong together and how different tasks flow throughout the year. As well, this guide provides helpful tips for determining where we are in the garden year without relying on a calendar; for instance, I always prepare my roses for a new year's growth by pruning them when the forsythia shrubs have begun to bloom their happy yellow. I plant my dahlia tubers when the soil is no longer cold and wet in my hand, exactly when the vegetable growers are setting out their tomatoes, but that date is a little different every year.

Part Four: Gather and Celebrate may come at the end of the book, but you could also think of it as a beginning. Reflecting on the harvests we most want and the moments in the garden year we hope to celebrate will drive all the decisions we make throughout the year. Do you want to grow flowers for a family wedding in September? Then you might choose pink dahlias and white cosmos seeds from the catalogs in January. Do you want to host a summer garden party in July? Then you will sow zinnia and sunflower seeds accordingly. In my own planner, I have noted the date when my heirloom rambler rose 'Albertine' blooms in late spring, and I have told my friends to expect a petal-dusted picnic round about the first of June. Truthfully, I am not much

for detailed planning and ambitious goal setting, but I love a garden year filled with good things to look forward to.

Most of all, I hope you will never see this book as a taskmaster or as a record of disappointments and failures. Instead, I hope you will circle round and round this book recording beauties observed, garden visions both unrealized and fulfilled, and, yes, failures (they are our best garden teachers!). When life feels dull or devoid of color, I hope this book will be the one you reach for to remember how many good gifts a garden year can give. I hope this journal will show you, in your own jotted notes and hasty sketches, that you have so much to anticipate. And when every page is filled up, I hope you will purchase another copy, pencil *Volume Two* on the title page, and keep on planning, keep on plotting, and always keep on planting. A flower garden life is a delightful life. And today is a good day to begin.

Gardening is not some sort of game by which one proves his superiority over others, nor is it a marketplace for the display of elegant things that others cannot afford. It is, on the contrary, a growing work of creation, endless in its changing elements. It is not a monument or an achievement, but a sort of traveling, a kind of pilgrimage you might say, often a bit grubby and sweaty though true pilgrims do not mind that. A garden is not a picture, but a language, which is of course the major art of life.

HENRY MITCHELL

The Essential Earthman

— PART ONE —

DREAM

If you believe that flower gardens must start with a visit to a plant store or by picking up a spade, I have good news for you. Gardens actually begin when we let ourselves dream. Beautiful flower gardens first spread their roots in our hearts and minds, and so Part One of this book is an invitation to forget about what's practical or reasonable or even possible and simply allow yourself to imagine a world with more creativity, more color, more life.

What do you envision when you let yourself freely dream about a garden? Perhaps you see a hand-tied bouquet as beautiful as a work of art. Perhaps you see a riotous meadow that draws swooping butterflies and zigzagging birds. Maybe you picture romantic roses and imagine their exquisite scent, or maybe you envision the garden party that takes place amongst the roses. When we dream of a garden, we dream of very particular delights. If the garden dreams in you are still fuzzy and haven't quite come into focus, spend time reflecting on the following questions.

Imagine a New Garden

Are there any flowers or gardens in my childhood memories?
Are there books or works of art related to gardens that I especially love?

Do I want a flower garden that is an inviting place to spend time, or do I want a garden designed for harvesting? Do I want an ornamental garden, a productive garden, or a little of both?

Which matters most to me: the overall picture my flower garden
makes or the individual flowers I grow in it?

How important is it to me that this garden provide food
and habitat for insects, birds, and other wildlife?

Is this a garden just for me, or will I share it with other adults, children, or pets?

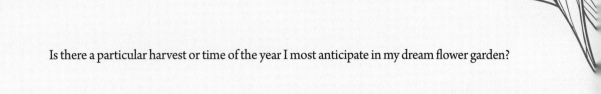

Is there a particular harvest or time of the year I most anticipate in my dream flower garden?

Do I have flexibility when it comes to locating my flower garden, or am I limited to a particular place with particular conditions?

The roots of our future gardens stretch far out behind us, sunk deep in a lifetime of stories and dreams.

CHRISTIE PURIFOY

Garden Maker

Most Loved Flowers

———

A list of favorites will be different for every gardener because we especially love those flowers that love to grow in our conditions. We gardeners do not simply impose our will on a place, because gardening is a relationship with a place. These, then, are my favorites for the gardens at Maplehurst in Pennsylvania. May they inspire your own unique garden dreams.

1. Dahlias, especially the water-lily types

2. Roses, especially David Austin's English roses

3. Lilies, especially scented oriental types

4. Hellebores, for late-winter beauty

5. Cosmos, for the way they dance in the summer wind

6. Zinnias, for thriving in summer heat

7. *Verbena bonariensis*, for generously multiplying themselves

BEAUTY FOR
Every Season

———

A flower garden planted for all four seasons is my favorite kind of calendar.
Instead of April or Monday, my garden tells me these are daffodil days or zinnia weeks.
And instead of winter, I have First Frost and Snow on the Seedheads.

1.   Include structure with paths, ornaments, buildings, and evergreen shrubs.
     The bare bones of a garden's structure can be beautiful in winter.

2.   Bulbs! Bulbs! Bulbs! Think beyond daffodils and tulips. Even the earliest spring
     days can be colorful with tiny bulbs like chionodoxa and scilla. Flowering bulbs
     can continue with allium, camassia, and autumn crocus.

3.   Think of every stage of your flowering plant's life. For instance, tall sedums like
     'Autumn Joy' emerge in spring as succulent rosettes that set off tulips
     beautifully. The seedheads of many coneflowers and ornamental grasses are
     visually stunning in autumn and winter.

4.   Color is possible in each season for most climates. Dogwood stems can be red
     and yellow, and conifers can be bronze. Hellebore, witch hazel, and daphne
     bloom even in cold weather.

5.   Think of your garden like a symphony. When does it go quiet? When is it loudest?
     Fill the gaps in time with early-blooming and late-blooming varieties of flowers
     you already grow.

WINTER

SPRING

These pages are for recording what is colorful, beautiful, or noteworthy in each season in your part of the world. Pay attention to your garden as well as to botanical gardens and neighborhood gardens. Study everything from flower and leaf color, to shape, to texture, and even the bark. You might like to take notes on a single perennial in every season, as they can change so much as they grow.

SUMMER

AUTUMN

YEAR TWO

WINTER

SPRING

YEAR TWO

SUMMER

AUTUMN

YEAR THREE

WINTER

SPRING

YEAR THREE

SUMMER

AUTUMN

YEAR FOUR

WINTER

SPRING

YEAR FOUR

SUMMER

AUTUMN

YEAR FIVE

WINTER

SPRING

YEAR FIVE

SUMMER

AUTUMN

HOW TO CRAFT A
Color Palette

———

1. Study paintings, make bouquets, take a look at the clothes in your closet: activities like these can help you see the colors you love the most. Gardens are personal.

2. Tone matters more than color. My warm purple dahlias look great with fiery orange cosmos, but my cool purple dahlias look better with pinks and blues.

3. White is not a neutral (it might have a cool blue tone or a creamy yellow tone), but it is incredibly useful. It draws attention to itself, shows up well in the shade, and can intensify other colors in the garden.

4. Familiarize yourself with the color wheel, but don't stress about it. Colors on opposite sides of the wheel will create an energetic combination. Using colors adjacent to one another on the wheel creates a calming effect.

5. Green is the color of health in a garden. While gold, silver, and red foliage can be great fun, too much can give even a colorful flower garden an unhealthy or unnatural appearance.

6. The beauty of accidental color combinations can be one of the great gifts of the flower garden. Pay attention to what the garden gives!

My Color
NOTES

These pages are yours to fill with all your dreams of color. You might take note of beautiful color combinations. You can sketch and doodle and play with colored pencils; you can add ribbon and fabric with glue. You might describe in words the colors of favorite flowers in order to create new combinations next year.

HOW TO CREATE
Beautiful Plant Combinations

———————

1. Color matters but contrast matters more. Study black-and-white photos of gardens you love, and you should see a dynamic composition rather than a monochromatic blur.

2. Flowers come in so many shapes. A garden with only pom-pom or daisy shapes will be less interesting than one with flowers in round, umbel, and spiky forms.

3. Remember texture. I learned to love the thick, wide leaves of hostas when I began planting them alongside the delicate foliage of ferns.

4. Observe all the colors in a plant, not only the colors of the petals. My dark pink cosmos look wonderful with sulfur-yellow bronze fennel because the center of each cosmos is the same golden yellow. The burgundy stems of emerging peonies look incredible alongside the pink of cherry blossom.

My Plant Pairing NOTES

Just as a sommelier takes notes on favorite wine and food pairings, use these pages for recording especially noteworthy garden combinations.

COMBINATION:

TIME(S) OF YEAR:

WHAT DO I LOVE ABOUT IT?

COMBINATION:

TIME(S) OF YEAR:

WHAT DO I LOVE ABOUT IT?

COMBINATION:

TIME(S) OF YEAR:

WHAT DO I LOVE ABOUT IT?

COMBINATION:

TIME(S) OF YEAR:

WHAT DO I LOVE ABOUT IT?

COMBINATION:

TIME(S) OF YEAR:

WHAT DO I LOVE ABOUT IT?

COMBINATION:

TIME(S) OF YEAR:

WHAT DO I LOVE ABOUT IT?

COMBINATION:

TIME(S) OF YEAR:

WHAT DO I LOVE ABOUT IT?

COMBINATION:

TIME(S) OF YEAR:

WHAT DO I LOVE ABOUT IT?

COMBINATION:

TIME(S) OF YEAR:

WHAT DO I LOVE ABOUT IT?

COMBINATION:

TIME(S) OF YEAR:

WHAT DO I LOVE ABOUT IT?

COMBINATION:

TIME(S) OF YEAR:

WHAT DO I LOVE ABOUT IT?

COMBINATION:

TIME(S) OF YEAR:

WHAT DO I LOVE ABOUT IT?

COMBINATION:

TIME(S) OF YEAR:

WHAT DO I LOVE ABOUT IT?

COMBINATION:

TIME(S) OF YEAR:

WHAT DO I LOVE ABOUT IT?

COMBINATION:

TIME(S) OF YEAR:

WHAT DO I LOVE ABOUT IT?

COMBINATION:

TIME(S) OF YEAR:

WHAT DO I LOVE ABOUT IT?

COMBINATION:

TIME(S) OF YEAR:

WHAT DO I LOVE ABOUT IT?

COMBINATION:

TIME(S) OF YEAR:

WHAT DO I LOVE ABOUT IT?

COMBINATION:

TIME(S) OF YEAR:

WHAT DO I LOVE ABOUT IT?

COMBINATION:

TIME(S) OF YEAR:

WHAT DO I LOVE ABOUT IT?

COMBINATION:

TIME(S) OF YEAR:

WHAT DO I LOVE ABOUT IT?

COMBINATION:

TIME(S) OF YEAR:

WHAT DO I LOVE ABOUT IT?

COMBINATION:

TIME(S) OF YEAR:

WHAT DO I LOVE ABOUT IT?

COMBINATION:

TIME(S) OF YEAR:

WHAT DO I LOVE ABOUT IT?

COMBINATION:

TIME(S) OF YEAR:

WHAT DO I LOVE ABOUT IT?

COMBINATION:

TIME(S) OF YEAR:

WHAT DO I LOVE ABOUT IT?

COMBINATION:

TIME(S) OF YEAR:

WHAT DO I LOVE ABOUT IT?

COMBINATION:

TIME(S) OF YEAR:

WHAT DO I LOVE ABOUT IT?

COMBINATION:

TIME(S) OF YEAR:

WHAT DO I LOVE ABOUT IT?

COMBINATION:

TIME(S) OF YEAR:

WHAT DO I LOVE ABOUT IT?

COMBINATION:

TIME(S) OF YEAR:

WHAT DO I LOVE ABOUT IT?

COMBINATION:

TIME(S) OF YEAR:

WHAT DO I LOVE ABOUT IT?

To Grow
SOMEDAY

See something wonderful?
Record it here. One day, you'll begin
a new garden, or simply a new garden
bed, and you can turn to this list for
ready-made planting ideas.

NAME AND / OR DESCRIPTION:

WHERE DID I SEE IT?

WHAT DO I LOVE ABOUT IT?

NAME AND / OR DESCRIPTION:

WHERE DID I SEE IT?

WHAT DO I LOVE ABOUT IT?

NAME AND / OR DESCRIPTION:

WHERE DID I SEE IT?

WHAT DO I LOVE ABOUT IT?

NAME AND / OR DESCRIPTION:

WHERE DID I SEE IT?

WHAT DO I LOVE ABOUT IT?

NAME AND / OR DESCRIPTION:

WHERE DID I SEE IT?

WHAT DO I LOVE ABOUT IT?

NAME AND / OR DESCRIPTION:

WHERE DID I SEE IT?

WHAT DO I LOVE ABOUT IT?

NAME AND / OR DESCRIPTION:

WHERE DID I SEE IT?

WHAT DO I LOVE ABOUT IT?

NAME AND / OR DESCRIPTION:

WHERE DID I SEE IT?

WHAT DO I LOVE ABOUT IT?

NAME AND / OR DESCRIPTION:

WHERE DID I SEE IT?

WHAT DO I LOVE ABOUT IT?

NAME AND / OR DESCRIPTION:

WHERE DID I SEE IT?

WHAT DO I LOVE ABOUT IT?

NAME AND / OR DESCRIPTION:

WHERE DID I SEE IT?

WHAT DO I LOVE ABOUT IT?

NAME AND / OR DESCRIPTION:

WHERE DID I SEE IT?

WHAT DO I LOVE ABOUT IT?

NAME AND / OR DESCRIPTION:

WHERE DID I SEE IT?

WHAT DO I LOVE ABOUT IT?

NAME AND / OR DESCRIPTION:

WHERE DID I SEE IT?

WHAT DO I LOVE ABOUT IT?

NAME AND / OR DESCRIPTION:

WHERE DID I SEE IT?

WHAT DO I LOVE ABOUT IT?

NAME AND / OR DESCRIPTION:

WHERE DID I SEE IT?

WHAT DO I LOVE ABOUT IT?

NAME AND / OR DESCRIPTION:

WHERE DID I SEE IT?

WHAT DO I LOVE ABOUT IT?

NAME AND / OR DESCRIPTION:

WHERE DID I SEE IT?

WHAT DO I LOVE ABOUT IT?

NAME AND / OR DESCRIPTION:

WHERE DID I SEE IT?

WHAT DO I LOVE ABOUT IT?

NAME AND / OR DESCRIPTION:

WHERE DID I SEE IT?

WHAT DO I LOVE ABOUT IT?

NAME AND / OR DESCRIPTION:

WHERE DID I SEE IT?

WHAT DO I LOVE ABOUT IT?

NAME AND / OR DESCRIPTION:

WHERE DID I SEE IT?

WHAT DO I LOVE ABOUT IT?

NAME AND / OR DESCRIPTION:

WHERE DID I SEE IT?

WHAT DO I LOVE ABOUT IT?

NAME AND / OR DESCRIPTION:

WHERE DID I SEE IT?

WHAT DO I LOVE ABOUT IT?

NAME AND / OR DESCRIPTION:

WHERE DID I SEE IT?

WHAT DO I LOVE ABOUT IT?

NAME AND / OR DESCRIPTION:

WHERE DID I SEE IT?

WHAT DO I LOVE ABOUT IT?

NAME AND / OR DESCRIPTION:

WHERE DID I SEE IT?

WHAT DO I LOVE ABOUT IT?

NAME AND / OR DESCRIPTION:

WHERE DID I SEE IT?

WHAT DO I LOVE ABOUT IT?

NAME AND / OR DESCRIPTION:

WHERE DID I SEE IT?

WHAT DO I LOVE ABOUT IT?

NAME AND / OR DESCRIPTION:

WHERE DID I SEE IT?

WHAT DO I LOVE ABOUT IT?

NAME AND / OR DESCRIPTION:

WHERE DID I SEE IT?

WHAT DO I LOVE ABOUT IT?

Happiness?
The color of it must
be spring green.

FRANCES MAYES

CHRISTIE'S
Garden Diary

My flower garden dream began because the empty space on the western front of the house seemed to beg for something colorful and beautiful. The flower garden was a vision of what emptiness could become. These days, I've been dreaming about a hidden garden down in the lowest corner of the property behind the house. This vision hasn't emerged from emptiness. Rather, it is my response to what the land already seems to be offering in that place. There is a circle of open grass surrounded by trees. If I fill in some of the gaps with more trees and shrubs, I could close that circle off entirely from sight. Only the initiated would know where to find the entrance hidden between the trunks of two towering Norway spruce trees. This fall I must remember to plant daffodils in the circle. They will give us a reason to visit this secret garden each spring.

PART TWO

PREPARE

Every gardener must learn to pay attention to the present, while remembering the past and anticipating the future. In that way, gardening is a lot like living. We must root ourselves in the present moment in order to stay steady, but we are even steadier when we look back with gratitude and forward with hope. This may sound abstract, but when we plan a garden, our thoughts quickly turn to the concrete stuff of gardening: soil, seeds, spades, and so forth. Gardening is both philosophical and practical. Again, like life.

To prepare for a new garden, or even for a new season in an old garden, we should consider our soil foremost. What areas of the garden need covering or feeding? Do I have material on hand, like cut grass or chopped leaves or homemade compost from a pile, or will I need to order a delivery of organic compost? What state are my tools in? What tools will I need to buy or borrow for the next season's work? If there is time, new planting areas can be prepared by laying down cardboard and topping it with a heavy mulch or compost. After a few months, the cardboard will have softened, and you can plant directly into it. No digging up of turf or weeds required.

HOW TO
Care for Soil

———

FEED IT:

Avoid synthetic fertilizers in favor of natural products like seaweed and fish emulsions, composted manure, and homemade compost; grass clippings left in place will feed the soil, as will disease-free garden debris.

COVER IT:

Use cardboard, newspaper, compost, and/or a mulch made from chopped leaves or wood.

STAY OFF OF IT AND OUT OF IT:

Don't be tempted to step onto raised beds; when working in freshly turned soil, walk on a board to distribute the weight of your feet. Instead of tilling and double digging, try gently layering compost on top to preserve the soil's own structure.

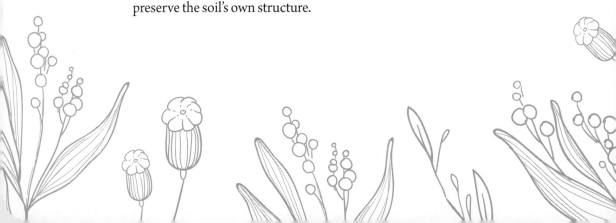

My Garden's Soil
NOTES

Use these pages to note which areas of your garden have been fed and covered—and with what material and when.

MY SOIL NOTES

MY SOIL NOTES

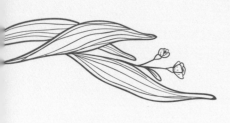

My Garden
GOALS

YEAR:	SEASON:
NOTES:	

YEAR:	SEASON:
NOTES:	

Here is space for clarifying your goals as a gardener. Though we may give practicalities little notice while we dream, we cannot ignore practicalities forever. Gardens are whimsical and beautiful, but they are imminently practical as well. Now is the time to ask, *What must I do in each season to reach the goals I have set for myself*? If you are allergic to the word *goals*, as I seem to be, try using gentler words like *focus* or *attention*. Few of us can attend to every garden dream in every season. *What will I choose to focus on next? What part of the garden or what aspect of gardening will receive my attention this year?*

YEAR: SEASON:

NOTES:

YEAR: SEASON:

NOTES:

YEAR: SEASON:

NOTES:

YEAR: SEASON:

NOTES:

YEAR: SEASON:

NOTES:

YEAR: SEASON:

NOTES:

YEAR: SEASON:

NOTES:

YEAR: SEASON:

NOTES:

YEAR: SEASON:

NOTES:

YEAR: SEASON:

NOTES:

YEAR: SEASON:

NOTES:

YEAR: SEASON:

NOTES:

YEAR: SEASON:

NOTES:

YEAR: SEASON:

NOTES:

YEAR: SEASON:

NOTES:

YEAR: SEASON:

NOTES:

YEAR: SEASON:

NOTES:

YEAR: SEASON:

NOTES:

Easiest Flowers to Grow from Seed

---

1. **ZINNIAS**: I especially love the 'Queen Lime' series and the 'Benary's Giant'.

2. **COSMOS**: most are tall, but more petite varieties like 'Apricot Lemonade' and 'Sulphur' are lovely.

3. **SWEET PEAS**: these can be planted directly in the soil in fall (for warmer climates) and late winter (for colder ones).

4. **SNAPDRAGONS**: I start mine early to get a jump on the season because these love to grow in cooler weather (can be planted in late fall for zone 7 and warmer).

5. **SUNFLOWERS**: these are easy to grow, but the largest can benefit from staking.

6. **(BONUS!) NASTURTIUM**: this cheerful flower works great in both salads and bouquets.

CHRISTIE'S
Bouquet Recipes

Beautiful homegrown bouquets are often serendipitous, but a little bit of planning can yield reliably beautiful arrangements. There are few things as sad as a cut flower garden full of flowers that seem to clash rather than harmonize. Here are a few tips and recipes for bouquets that sing.

SPRING RECIPE:

'Chantilly Light Salmon' snapdragons + bronze fennel foliage + orlaya

EARLY SUMMER RECIPE:

pale pink roses + 'Southern Charm' verbascum + ninebark foliage
(For pink roses I like David Austin's 'Gentle Hermione')

LATE SUMMER RECIPE:

yellow sunflowers + feverfew + leafy green filler
(I like 'Sunfinity' sunflowers and to raid the herb garden for the filler)

AUTUMN RECIPE:

'Queen Red Lime' zinnias + panicle hydrangeas + fountain grass + goldenrod
(The lime flowers from 'Limelight' or the burgundy of 'Fire Light' are especially good and the goldenrod brings out the yellow at the center of the zinnia)

My Bouquet
RECIPES

ARRANGEMENT NAME OR THEME:

SEASON:

PLANTS INCLUDED:

ARRANGEMENT NAME OR THEME:

SEASON:

PLANTS INCLUDED:

ARRANGEMENT NAME OR THEME:

SEASON:

PLANTS INCLUDED:

ARRANGEMENT NAME OR THEME:

SEASON:

PLANTS INCLUDED:

ARRANGEMENT NAME OR THEME:

SEASON:

PLANTS INCLUDED:

ARRANGEMENT NAME OR THEME:

SEASON:

PLANTS INCLUDED:

ARRANGEMENT NAME OR THEME:

SEASON:

PLANTS INCLUDED:

ARRANGEMENT NAME OR THEME:

SEASON:

PLANTS INCLUDED:

ARRANGEMENT NAME OR THEME:

SEASON:

PLANTS INCLUDED:

ARRANGEMENT NAME OR THEME:

SEASON:

PLANTS INCLUDED:

ARRANGEMENT NAME OR THEME:

SEASON:

PLANTS INCLUDED:

ARRANGEMENT NAME OR THEME:

SEASON:

PLANTS INCLUDED:

ARRANGEMENT NAME OR THEME:

SEASON:

PLANTS INCLUDED:

ARRANGEMENT NAME OR THEME:

SEASON:

PLANTS INCLUDED:

ARRANGEMENT NAME OR THEME:

SEASON:

PLANTS INCLUDED:

ARRANGEMENT NAME OR THEME:

SEASON:

PLANTS INCLUDED:

ARRANGEMENT NAME OR THEME:

SEASON:

PLANTS INCLUDED:

ARRANGEMENT NAME OR THEME:

SEASON:

PLANTS INCLUDED:

ARRANGEMENT NAME OR THEME:

SEASON:

PLANTS INCLUDED:

ARRANGEMENT NAME OR THEME:

SEASON:

PLANTS INCLUDED:

ARRANGEMENT NAME OR THEME:

SEASON:

PLANTS INCLUDED:

ARRANGEMENT NAME OR THEME:

SEASON:

PLANTS INCLUDED:

ARRANGEMENT NAME OR THEME:

SEASON:

PLANTS INCLUDED:

ARRANGEMENT NAME OR THEME:

SEASON:

PLANTS INCLUDED:

ARRANGEMENT NAME OR THEME:

SEASON:

PLANTS INCLUDED:

ARRANGEMENT NAME OR THEME:

SEASON:

PLANTS INCLUDED:

ARRANGEMENT NAME OR THEME:

SEASON:

PLANTS INCLUDED:

ARRANGEMENT NAME OR THEME:

SEASON:

PLANTS INCLUDED:

ARRANGEMENT NAME OR THEME:

SEASON:

PLANTS INCLUDED:

ARRANGEMENT NAME OR THEME:

SEASON:

PLANTS INCLUDED:

ARRANGEMENT NAME OR THEME:

SEASON:

PLANTS INCLUDED:

ARRANGEMENT NAME OR THEME:

SEASON:

PLANTS INCLUDED:

ARRANGEMENT NAME OR THEME:

SEASON:

PLANTS INCLUDED:

ARRANGEMENT NAME OR THEME:

SEASON:

PLANTS INCLUDED:

ARRANGEMENT NAME OR THEME:

SEASON:

PLANTS INCLUDED:

ARRANGEMENT NAME OR THEME:

SEASON:

PLANTS INCLUDED:

ARRANGEMENT NAME OR THEME:

SEASON:

PLANTS INCLUDED:

ARRANGEMENT NAME OR THEME:

SEASON:

PLANTS INCLUDED:

ARRANGEMENT NAME OR THEME:

SEASON:

PLANTS INCLUDED:

ARRANGEMENT NAME OR THEME:

SEASON:

PLANTS INCLUDED:

A Record of My
SEEDS

Use these pages to take notes on your garden seeds: when you ordered them, where you purchased them, how you planted them, and whether they were sown indoors or directly into the garden.

NAME OF PLANT:

DATE ORDERED: /   /   SOURCE:

NOTES ON SOWING:

NAME OF PLANT:

DATE ORDERED: /   /   SOURCE:

NOTES ON SOWING:

NAME OF PLANT:

DATE ORDERED: /   /   SOURCE:

NOTES ON SOWING:

NAME OF PLANT:

DATE ORDERED: /   /   SOURCE:

NOTES ON SOWING:

NAME OF PLANT:

DATE ORDERED: /   /   SOURCE:

NOTES ON SOWING:

NAME OF PLANT:

DATE ORDERED: /   /   SOURCE:

NOTES ON SOWING:

NAME OF PLANT:

DATE ORDERED: /   /   SOURCE:

NOTES ON SOWING:

NAME OF PLANT:

DATE ORDERED: /   /   SOURCE:

NOTES ON SOWING:

NAME OF PLANT:

DATE ORDERED: /   /   SOURCE:

NOTES ON SOWING:

NAME OF PLANT:

DATE ORDERED: /   /   SOURCE:

NOTES ON SOWING:

NAME OF PLANT:

DATE ORDERED: /   /   SOURCE:

NOTES ON SOWING:

NAME OF PLANT:

DATE ORDERED: /   /   SOURCE:

NOTES ON SOWING:

NAME OF PLANT:

DATE ORDERED: /   /   SOURCE:

NOTES ON SOWING:

NAME OF PLANT:

DATE ORDERED: /   /   SOURCE:

NOTES ON SOWING:

NAME OF PLANT:

DATE ORDERED: /   /   SOURCE:

NOTES ON SOWING:

NAME OF PLANT:

DATE ORDERED: /   /   SOURCE:

NOTES ON SOWING:

NAME OF PLANT:

DATE ORDERED: /   /   SOURCE:

NOTES ON SOWING:

NAME OF PLANT:

DATE ORDERED: /   /   SOURCE:

NOTES ON SOWING:

NAME OF PLANT:

DATE ORDERED: /   /   SOURCE:

NOTES ON SOWING:

NAME OF PLANT:

DATE ORDERED: / / SOURCE:

NOTES ON SOWING:

NAME OF PLANT:

DATE ORDERED: / / SOURCE:

NOTES ON SOWING:

NAME OF PLANT:

DATE ORDERED: / / SOURCE:

NOTES ON SOWING:

NAME OF PLANT:

DATE ORDERED: / / SOURCE:

NOTES ON SOWING:

NAME OF PLANT:

DATE ORDERED: / / SOURCE:

NOTES ON SOWING:

NAME OF PLANT:

DATE ORDERED: / / SOURCE:

NOTES ON SOWING:

NAME OF PLANT:

DATE ORDERED: / / SOURCE:

NOTES ON SOWING:

NAME OF PLANT:

DATE ORDERED: / / SOURCE:

NOTES ON SOWING:

NAME OF PLANT:

DATE ORDERED: / / SOURCE:

NOTES ON SOWING:

NAME OF PLANT:

DATE ORDERED: / / SOURCE:

NOTES ON SOWING:

NAME OF PLANT:

DATE ORDERED: /   /   SOURCE:

NOTES ON SOWING:

NAME OF PLANT:

DATE ORDERED: /   /   SOURCE:

NOTES ON SOWING:

NAME OF PLANT:

DATE ORDERED: /   /   SOURCE:

NOTES ON SOWING:

NAME OF PLANT:

DATE ORDERED: /   /   SOURCE:

NOTES ON SOWING:

NAME OF PLANT:

DATE ORDERED: /   /   SOURCE:

NOTES ON SOWING:

NAME OF PLANT:

DATE ORDERED: /   /   SOURCE:

NOTES ON SOWING:

NAME OF PLANT:

DATE ORDERED: /   /   SOURCE:

NOTES ON SOWING:

NAME OF PLANT:

DATE ORDERED: /   /   SOURCE:

NOTES ON SOWING:

NAME OF PLANT:

DATE ORDERED: /   /   SOURCE:

NOTES ON SOWING:

NAME OF PLANT:

DATE ORDERED: /   /   SOURCE:

NOTES ON SOWING:

NAME OF PLANT:

DATE ORDERED: /   /   SOURCE:

NOTES ON SOWING:

NAME OF PLANT:

DATE ORDERED: /   /   SOURCE:

NOTES ON SOWING:

NAME OF PLANT:

DATE ORDERED: /   /   SOURCE:

NOTES ON SOWING:

NAME OF PLANT:

DATE ORDERED: /   /   SOURCE:

NOTES ON SOWING:

NAME OF PLANT:

DATE ORDERED: /   /   SOURCE:

NOTES ON SOWING:

NAME OF PLANT:

DATE ORDERED: / / SOURCE:

NOTES ON SOWING:

NAME OF PLANT:

DATE ORDERED: / / SOURCE:

NOTES ON SOWING:

NAME OF PLANT:

DATE ORDERED: / / SOURCE:

NOTES ON SOWING:

NAME OF PLANT:

DATE ORDERED: / / SOURCE:

NOTES ON SOWING:

NAME OF PLANT:

DATE ORDERED: / / SOURCE:

NOTES ON SOWING:

NAME OF PLANT:

DATE ORDERED: /   /   SOURCE:

NOTES ON SOWING:

NAME OF PLANT:

DATE ORDERED: /   /   SOURCE:

NOTES ON SOWING:

NAME OF PLANT:

DATE ORDERED: /   /   SOURCE:

NOTES ON SOWING:

NAME OF PLANT:

DATE ORDERED: /   /   SOURCE:

NOTES ON SOWING:

NAME OF PLANT:

DATE ORDERED: /   /   SOURCE:

NOTES ON SOWING:

NAME OF PLANT:

DATE ORDERED: /   /   SOURCE:

NOTES ON SOWING:

NAME OF PLANT:

DATE ORDERED: /   /   SOURCE:

NOTES ON SOWING:

NAME OF PLANT:

DATE ORDERED: /   /   SOURCE:

NOTES ON SOWING:

NAME OF PLANT:

DATE ORDERED: /   /   SOURCE:

NOTES ON SOWING:

NAME OF PLANT:

DATE ORDERED: /   /   SOURCE:

NOTES ON SOWING:

The gardener must put some kind of twist on the existing landscape, turn its prose into something nearer poetry.

MICHAEL POLLAN

Second Nature

GARDEN DESIGN TIPS
from Maplehurst

———

1. Be realistic and generous. Paths and beds should probably be wider than you first suppose, and you will likely need more plants than you think you will. My own garden requires daffodil bulbs by the hundreds and ornamental grasses by the dozens.

2. Pay attention to entrances, exits, paths, sight lines, and the views from your home's doors and windows. I might plant a beautiful little tree outside my dining room window this year.

3. Remember you are creating spaces in which to *be* as well as pretty pictures to see, which is why I removed the central planting bed in my flower garden and replaced it with a table and chairs.

4. Consider maintenance. Productive gardens and gardens filled with herbaceous perennials tend to require the most care while ornamental gardens composed mostly of trees and shrubs demand the least. My own flower garden now has many more shrubs and far fewer annuals than it once did.

5. Fill your garden's layers to visually connect tall plants (whether they are tall as trees or simply tall flowers) with the plants at ground level. The dogwood trees stand tall in my circular driveway bed, while baptisias help connect their height with the prairie dropseed grasses at the ground.

6. Consider microclimates. Is there a place sheltered from winter winds? Is there a low spot where frost pools? Where does the snow melt first in spring?

My Garden
PLOTTING

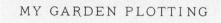

MY GARDEN PLOTTING

MY GARDEN PLOTTING

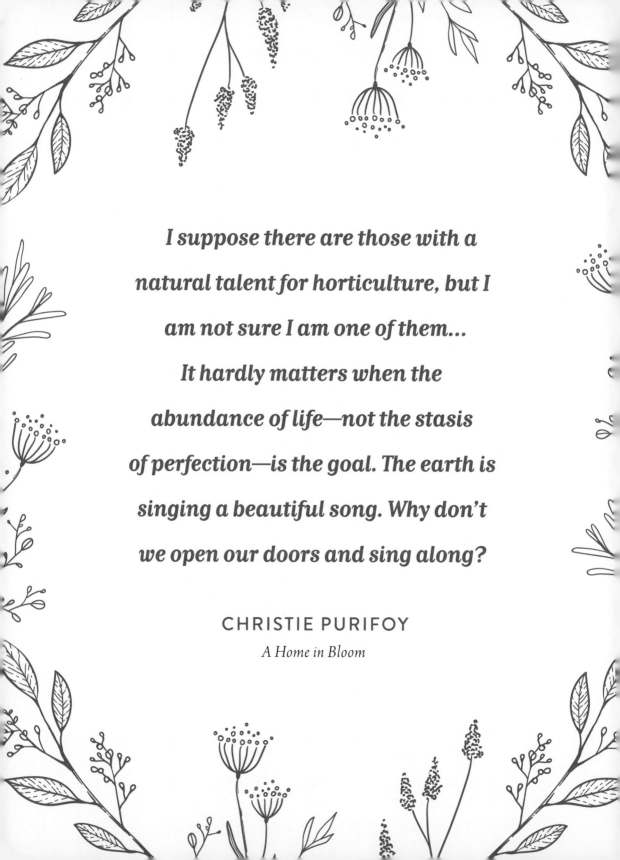

I suppose there are those with a

natural talent for horticulture, but I

am not sure I am one of them...

It hardly matters when the

abundance of life—not the stasis

of perfection—is the goal. The earth is

singing a beautiful song. Why don't

we open our doors and sing along?

CHRISTIE PURIFOY

A Home in Bloom

—— CHRISTIE'S ——

Garden Diary

Now that it is autumn, I have asked my husband to ride our lawn mower over all of our fallen leaves. I will cover the raised beds with blankets of chopped leaves. I will rake chopped leaves into all the planting beds. I went for a long drive to admire the colorful fall foliage and noticed the purple asters blooming in so many of my neighbors' gardens. Why don't I have these in my garden? I will walk around today and make a note of spots where asters might like to grow here at Maplehurst. Or could I find room for an aromatic aster hedge?

PART THREE

SOW, PLANT & TEND

If you are new to gardening and feel intimidated when you contemplate the work involved in caring for plants, I understand. The art of gardening is not like the art of painting. In order to paint beautiful pictures in our garden, we cannot simply reach out our hands for tubes labeled "ochre" or "vermilion." Instead, we must become intimate with a staggering array of plant material that may or may not be suited to our gardens.

But take heart. The path of learning in a garden is paved with beauty. You will cultivate glory and sow wonder even as you make errors and kill plants and learn from your mistakes and begin again. Unlike so many aspects of modern life—where productivity is all and what matters most are the widgets we churn out—gardening emphasizes the process. Gardeners are not those who have lovely gardens outside their door. Gardeners are those who are garden*ing*. And the delight of gardening is found precisely there— in the *–ing*. Gardens are never finished, but when the soil feels rich in our hands, when the sun is warm on our backs, when we greet the springtime return of our flowers like old friends, we can be truly glad that our gardens invite our ongoing participation. May the following pages record lessons learned and tasks accomplished as well as endless moments of delight.

Garden Tasks

The garden has no calendar. It pays no attention to the precision of our labels for days, weeks, and months. But every garden has a rhythm, as regular as breathing, and the following tasks are the inhale and exhale of my garden.

EARLY WINTER

✓ Order seeds for annual flowers like zinnias, cosmos, and sunflowers.

✓ Order dahlia tubers and bare-root roses.

LATE WINTER

✓ Sow seeds indoors for flowers that prefer cool spring weather (like snapdragons and alyssum).

✓ Plant bare-root roses as soon as the ground can be worked.

✓ Direct-sow sweet pea seeds.

EARLY SPRING

✓ Prune roses when the yellow forsythia shrubs bloom.

✓ Cut back last year's dead growth on the perennials and ornamental grasses (leave in place or add to compost pile).

MID-SPRING

✓ Sow seeds indoors for flowers that prefer warm weather (like zinnias).

✓ Photograph flowering bulb displays to help determine which new bulbs to order.

✓ Divide summer -and fall-blooming perennials that weren't divided in fall.

LATE SPRING

✓ Weed, weed, and weed some more. This may be the most important task of spring.

✓ Order flowering spring bulbs now, and they will be shipped at the right time for planting in fall.

✓ Plant dahlia tubers when the soil has warmed.

EARLY SUMMER

- ✓ Practice the "Chelsea chop" method of pruning on tall perennials: I always cut back my tall 'Jeana' phlox by at least a third so it stays upright when it flowers later in summer.

- ✓ Decide on a weekly schedule for watering and feeding containers ("Friday Feed" is my memory aid).

- ✓ Start another round of seeds for those annuals that might not last all summer (I love to plant out young zinnias and cosmos in midsummer for fresh flowers in late summer and early fall).

SUMMER

- ✓ Deadhead repeat-blooming roses and annual flowers regularly for more bloom.

- ✓ Start seeds of biennial flowers for fall planting (foxglove, verbascum, hollyhock).

- ✓ Divide bearded irises after they have finished flowering.

LATE SUMMER

- ✓ Enjoy the garden.

- ✓ Take a vacation (just ask a neighbor to water your containers and harvest your flowers while you're away!).

- ✓ Move peonies, if necessary.

EARLY FALL

- ✓ Planting time! Trees, shrubs, and perennials planted in fall will be well established to grow well in spring.
- ✓ Search out end-of-season sales in garden centers.
- ✓ Subscribe to mailing lists: seed and plant catalogs will ship soon!

MID-FALL

- ✓ Plant bulbs for spring flowers like tulips, daffodils, and crocuses.
- ✓ Look for clearance-priced trees and shrubs at garden centers (it is expensive for a nursery business to care for those over winter).

LATE FALL AND EARLY WINTER

- ✓ Plant amaryllis bulbs for indoor flowers.
- ✓ Continue planting bulbs, dividing and planting perennials, and planting shrubs and trees until the ground freezes.
- ✓ If zone 6b or colder, dig up dahlia tubers for storage once the foliage has blackened from cold.
- ✓ Prune back unsightly hostas, daylilies, and peonies after the first hard freeze.

A Record of My
GARDEN TASKS

Make special note of those tasks that seem to fit together, and which tasks must precede or follow others.

- [ ]
- [ ]
- [ ]
- [ ]
- [ ]
- [ ]
- [ ]
- [ ]
- [ ]
- [ ]
- [ ]
- [ ]
- [ ]
- [ ]
- [ ]
- [ ]
- [ ]
- [ ]
- [ ]
- [ ]
- [ ]
- [ ]

MY GARDEN TASKS

MY GARDEN TASKS

MY GARDEN TASKS

MY GARDEN TASKS

- [ ] _____
- [ ] _____
- [ ] _____
- [ ] _____
- [ ] _____
- [ ] _____
- [ ] _____
- [ ] _____
- [ ] _____
- [ ] _____
- [ ] _____
- [ ] _____
- [ ] _____
- [ ] _____
- [ ] _____
- [ ] _____
- [ ] _____
- [ ] _____
- [ ] _____
- [ ] _____
- [ ] _____
- [ ] _____
- [ ] _____
- [ ] _____
- [ ] _____
- [ ] _____

MY GARDEN TASKS

MY GARDEN TASKS

- [ ]
- [ ]
- [ ]
- [ ]
- [ ]
- [ ]
- [ ]
- [ ]
- [ ]
- [ ]
- [ ]
- [ ]
- [ ]
- [ ]
- [ ]
- [ ]
- [ ]
- [ ]
- [ ]
- [ ]
- [ ]
- [ ]
- [ ]
- [ ]
- [ ]
- [ ]
- [ ]

MY GARDEN TASKS

- [ ]
- [ ]
- [ ]
- [ ]
- [ ]
- [ ]
- [ ]
- [ ]
- [ ]
- [ ]
- [ ]
- [ ]
- [ ]
- [ ]
- [ ]
- [ ]
- [ ]
- [ ]
- [ ]
- [ ]
- [ ]
- [ ]
- [ ]
- [ ]
- [ ]
- [ ]
- [ ]

MY GARDEN TASKS

A Record of My
FLOWERS

SCIENTIFIC NAME AND VARIETY:

COMMON NAME:

NOTES ON CARE:

NOTES ON LOCATION:

SCIENTIFIC NAME AND VARIETY:

COMMON NAME:

NOTES ON CARE:

NOTES ON LOCATION:

SCIENTIFIC NAME AND VARIETY:

COMMON NAME:

NOTES ON CARE:

NOTES ON LOCATION:

SCIENTIFIC NAME AND VARIETY:

COMMON NAME:

NOTES ON CARE:

NOTES ON LOCATION:

SCIENTIFIC NAME AND VARIETY:

COMMON NAME:

NOTES ON CARE:

NOTES ON LOCATION:

SCIENTIFIC NAME AND VARIETY:

COMMON NAME:

NOTES ON CARE:

NOTES ON LOCATION:

SCIENTIFIC NAME AND VARIETY:

COMMON NAME:

NOTES ON CARE:

NOTES ON LOCATION:

SCIENTIFIC NAME AND VARIETY:

COMMON NAME:

NOTES ON CARE:

NOTES ON LOCATION:

SCIENTIFIC NAME AND VARIETY:

COMMON NAME:

NOTES ON CARE:

NOTES ON LOCATION:

SCIENTIFIC NAME AND VARIETY:

COMMON NAME:

NOTES ON CARE:

NOTES ON LOCATION:

SCIENTIFIC NAME AND VARIETY:

COMMON NAME:

NOTES ON CARE:

NOTES ON LOCATION:

SCIENTIFIC NAME AND VARIETY:

COMMON NAME:

NOTES ON CARE:

NOTES ON LOCATION:

SCIENTIFIC NAME AND VARIETY:

COMMON NAME:

NOTES ON CARE:

NOTES ON LOCATION:

SCIENTIFIC NAME AND VARIETY:

COMMON NAME:

NOTES ON CARE:

NOTES ON LOCATION:

SCIENTIFIC NAME AND VARIETY:

COMMON NAME:

NOTES ON CARE:

NOTES ON LOCATION:

SCIENTIFIC NAME AND VARIETY:

COMMON NAME:

NOTES ON CARE:

NOTES ON LOCATION:

SCIENTIFIC NAME AND VARIETY:

COMMON NAME:

NOTES ON CARE:

NOTES ON LOCATION:

SCIENTIFIC NAME AND VARIETY:

COMMON NAME:

NOTES ON CARE:

NOTES ON LOCATION:

SCIENTIFIC NAME AND VARIETY:

COMMON NAME:

NOTES ON CARE:

NOTES ON LOCATION:

SCIENTIFIC NAME AND VARIETY:

COMMON NAME:

NOTES ON CARE:

NOTES ON LOCATION:

SCIENTIFIC NAME AND VARIETY:

COMMON NAME:

NOTES ON CARE:

NOTES ON LOCATION:

SCIENTIFIC NAME AND VARIETY:

COMMON NAME:

NOTES ON CARE:

NOTES ON LOCATION:

SCIENTIFIC NAME AND VARIETY:

COMMON NAME:

NOTES ON CARE:

NOTES ON LOCATION:

SCIENTIFIC NAME AND VARIETY:

COMMON NAME:

NOTES ON CARE:

NOTES ON LOCATION:

SCIENTIFIC NAME AND VARIETY:

COMMON NAME:

NOTES ON CARE:

NOTES ON LOCATION:

SCIENTIFIC NAME AND VARIETY:

COMMON NAME:

NOTES ON CARE:

NOTES ON LOCATION:

SCIENTIFIC NAME AND VARIETY:

COMMON NAME:

NOTES ON CARE:

NOTES ON LOCATION:

SCIENTIFIC NAME AND VARIETY:

COMMON NAME:

NOTES ON CARE:

NOTES ON LOCATION:

SCIENTIFIC NAME AND VARIETY:

COMMON NAME:

NOTES ON CARE:

NOTES ON LOCATION:

SCIENTIFIC NAME AND VARIETY:

COMMON NAME:

NOTES ON CARE:

NOTES ON LOCATION:

SCIENTIFIC NAME AND VARIETY:

COMMON NAME:

NOTES ON CARE:

NOTES ON LOCATION:

SCIENTIFIC NAME AND VARIETY:

COMMON NAME:

NOTES ON CARE:

NOTES ON LOCATION:

SCIENTIFIC NAME AND VARIETY:

COMMON NAME:

NOTES ON CARE:

NOTES ON LOCATION:

SCIENTIFIC NAME AND VARIETY:

COMMON NAME:

NOTES ON CARE:

NOTES ON LOCATION:

SCIENTIFIC NAME AND VARIETY:

COMMON NAME:

NOTES ON CARE:

NOTES ON LOCATION:

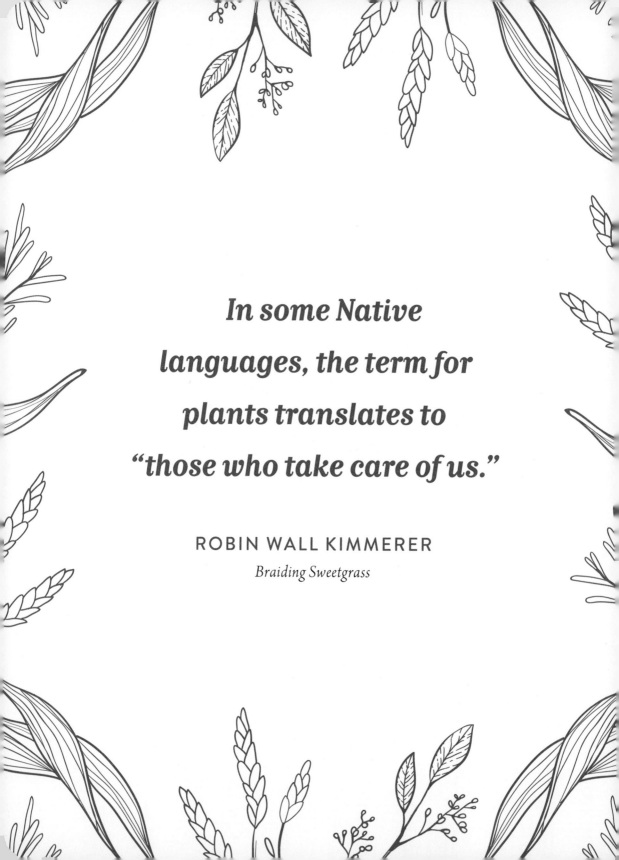

In some Native languages, the term for plants translates to "those who take care of us."

ROBIN WALL KIMMERER

Braiding Sweetgrass

SCIENTIFIC NAME AND VARIETY:

COMMON NAME:

NOTES ON CARE:

NOTES ON LOCATION:

SCIENTIFIC NAME AND VARIETY:

COMMON NAME:

NOTES ON CARE:

NOTES ON LOCATION:

SCIENTIFIC NAME AND VARIETY:

COMMON NAME:

NOTES ON CARE:

NOTES ON LOCATION:

SCIENTIFIC NAME AND VARIETY:

COMMON NAME:

NOTES ON CARE:

NOTES ON LOCATION:

SCIENTIFIC NAME AND VARIETY:

COMMON NAME:

NOTES ON CARE:

NOTES ON LOCATION:

SCIENTIFIC NAME AND VARIETY:

COMMON NAME:

NOTES ON CARE:

NOTES ON LOCATION:

SCIENTIFIC NAME AND VARIETY:

COMMON NAME:

NOTES ON CARE:

NOTES ON LOCATION:

SCIENTIFIC NAME AND VARIETY:

COMMON NAME:

NOTES ON CARE:

NOTES ON LOCATION:

SCIENTIFIC NAME AND VARIETY:

COMMON NAME:

NOTES ON CARE:

NOTES ON LOCATION:

SCIENTIFIC NAME AND VARIETY:

COMMON NAME:

NOTES ON CARE:

NOTES ON LOCATION:

SCIENTIFIC NAME AND VARIETY:

COMMON NAME:

NOTES ON CARE:

NOTES ON LOCATION:

SCIENTIFIC NAME AND VARIETY:

COMMON NAME:

NOTES ON CARE:

NOTES ON LOCATION:

SCIENTIFIC NAME AND VARIETY:

COMMON NAME:

NOTES ON CARE:

NOTES ON LOCATION:

SCIENTIFIC NAME AND VARIETY:

COMMON NAME:

NOTES ON CARE:

NOTES ON LOCATION:

SCIENTIFIC NAME AND VARIETY:

COMMON NAME:

NOTES ON CARE:

NOTES ON LOCATION:

SCIENTIFIC NAME AND VARIETY:

COMMON NAME:

NOTES ON CARE:

NOTES ON LOCATION:

SCIENTIFIC NAME AND VARIETY:

COMMON NAME:

NOTES ON CARE:

NOTES ON LOCATION:

SCIENTIFIC NAME AND VARIETY:

COMMON NAME:

NOTES ON CARE:

NOTES ON LOCATION:

SCIENTIFIC NAME AND VARIETY:

COMMON NAME:

NOTES ON CARE:

NOTES ON LOCATION:

SCIENTIFIC NAME AND VARIETY:

COMMON NAME:

NOTES ON CARE:

NOTES ON LOCATION:

SCIENTIFIC NAME AND VARIETY:

COMMON NAME:

NOTES ON CARE:

NOTES ON LOCATION:

SCIENTIFIC NAME AND VARIETY:

COMMON NAME:

NOTES ON CARE:

NOTES ON LOCATION:

SCIENTIFIC NAME AND VARIETY:

COMMON NAME:

NOTES ON CARE:

NOTES ON LOCATION:

SCIENTIFIC NAME AND VARIETY:

COMMON NAME:

NOTES ON CARE:

NOTES ON LOCATION:

SCIENTIFIC NAME AND VARIETY:

COMMON NAME:

NOTES ON CARE:

NOTES ON LOCATION:

SCIENTIFIC NAME AND VARIETY:

COMMON NAME:

NOTES ON CARE:

NOTES ON LOCATION:

SCIENTIFIC NAME AND VARIETY:

COMMON NAME:

NOTES ON CARE:

NOTES ON LOCATION:

SCIENTIFIC NAME AND VARIETY:

COMMON NAME:

NOTES ON CARE:

NOTES ON LOCATION:

SCIENTIFIC NAME AND VARIETY:

COMMON NAME:

NOTES ON CARE:

NOTES ON LOCATION:

SCIENTIFIC NAME AND VARIETY:

COMMON NAME:

NOTES ON CARE:

NOTES ON LOCATION:

SCIENTIFIC NAME AND VARIETY:

COMMON NAME:

NOTES ON CARE:

NOTES ON LOCATION:

SCIENTIFIC NAME AND VARIETY:

COMMON NAME:

NOTES ON CARE:

NOTES ON LOCATION:

SCIENTIFIC NAME AND VARIETY:

COMMON NAME:

NOTES ON CARE:

NOTES ON LOCATION:

SCIENTIFIC NAME AND VARIETY:

COMMON NAME:

NOTES ON CARE:

NOTES ON LOCATION:

SCIENTIFIC NAME AND VARIETY:

COMMON NAME:

NOTES ON CARE:

NOTES ON LOCATION:

SCIENTIFIC NAME AND VARIETY:

COMMON NAME:

NOTES ON CARE:

NOTES ON LOCATION:

SCIENTIFIC NAME AND VARIETY:

COMMON NAME:

NOTES ON CARE:

NOTES ON LOCATION:

SCIENTIFIC NAME AND VARIETY:

COMMON NAME:

NOTES ON CARE:

NOTES ON LOCATION:

SCIENTIFIC NAME AND VARIETY:

COMMON NAME:

NOTES ON CARE:

NOTES ON LOCATION:

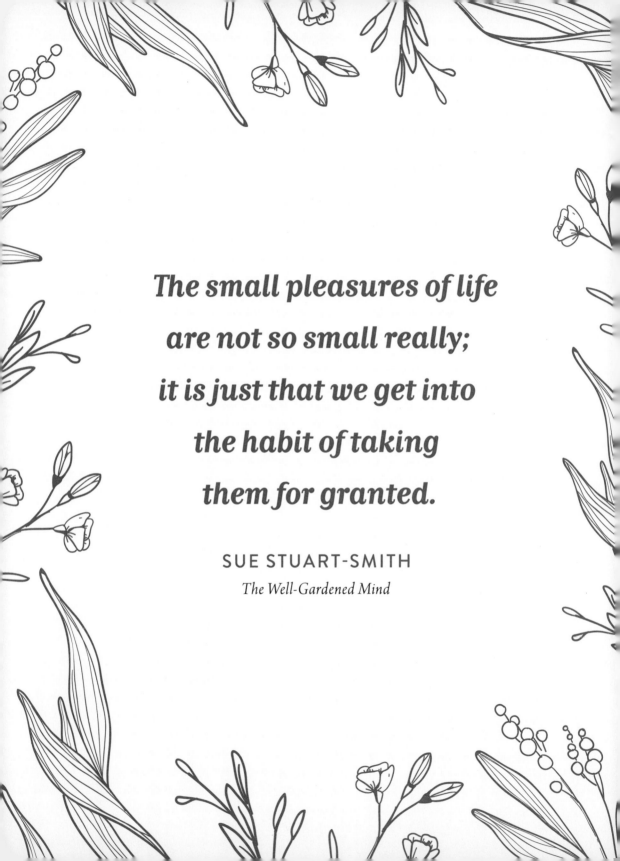

*The small pleasures of life
are not so small really;
it is just that we get into
the habit of taking
them for granted.*

SUE STUART-SMITH

The Well-Gardened Mind

SCIENTIFIC NAME AND VARIETY:

COMMON NAME:

NOTES ON CARE:

NOTES ON LOCATION:

SCIENTIFIC NAME AND VARIETY:

COMMON NAME:

NOTES ON CARE:

NOTES ON LOCATION:

SCIENTIFIC NAME AND VARIETY:

COMMON NAME:

NOTES ON CARE:

NOTES ON LOCATION:

SCIENTIFIC NAME AND VARIETY:

COMMON NAME:

NOTES ON CARE:

NOTES ON LOCATION:

SCIENTIFIC NAME AND VARIETY:

COMMON NAME:

NOTES ON CARE:

NOTES ON LOCATION:

SCIENTIFIC NAME AND VARIETY:

COMMON NAME:

NOTES ON CARE:

NOTES ON LOCATION:

SCIENTIFIC NAME AND VARIETY:

COMMON NAME:

NOTES ON CARE:

NOTES ON LOCATION:

SCIENTIFIC NAME AND VARIETY:

COMMON NAME:

NOTES ON CARE:

NOTES ON LOCATION:

SCIENTIFIC NAME AND VARIETY:

COMMON NAME:

NOTES ON CARE:

NOTES ON LOCATION:

SCIENTIFIC NAME AND VARIETY:

COMMON NAME:

NOTES ON CARE:

NOTES ON LOCATION:

SCIENTIFIC NAME AND VARIETY:

COMMON NAME:

NOTES ON CARE:

NOTES ON LOCATION:

SCIENTIFIC NAME AND VARIETY:

COMMON NAME:

NOTES ON CARE:

NOTES ON LOCATION:

SCIENTIFIC NAME AND VARIETY:

COMMON NAME:

NOTES ON CARE:

NOTES ON LOCATION:

SCIENTIFIC NAME AND VARIETY:

COMMON NAME:

NOTES ON CARE:

NOTES ON LOCATION:

SCIENTIFIC NAME AND VARIETY:

COMMON NAME:

NOTES ON CARE:

NOTES ON LOCATION:

SCIENTIFIC NAME AND VARIETY:

COMMON NAME:

NOTES ON CARE:

NOTES ON LOCATION:

SCIENTIFIC NAME AND VARIETY:

COMMON NAME:

NOTES ON CARE:

NOTES ON LOCATION:

SCIENTIFIC NAME AND VARIETY:

COMMON NAME:

NOTES ON CARE:

NOTES ON LOCATION:

SCIENTIFIC NAME AND VARIETY:

COMMON NAME:

NOTES ON CARE:

NOTES ON LOCATION:

SCIENTIFIC NAME AND VARIETY:

COMMON NAME:

NOTES ON CARE:

NOTES ON LOCATION:

SCIENTIFIC NAME AND VARIETY:

COMMON NAME:

NOTES ON CARE:

NOTES ON LOCATION:

SCIENTIFIC NAME AND VARIETY:

COMMON NAME:

NOTES ON CARE:

NOTES ON LOCATION:

SCIENTIFIC NAME AND VARIETY:

COMMON NAME:

NOTES ON CARE:

NOTES ON LOCATION:

SCIENTIFIC NAME AND VARIETY:

COMMON NAME:

NOTES ON CARE:

NOTES ON LOCATION:

SCIENTIFIC NAME AND VARIETY:

COMMON NAME:

NOTES ON CARE:

NOTES ON LOCATION:

SCIENTIFIC NAME AND VARIETY:

COMMON NAME:

NOTES ON CARE:

NOTES ON LOCATION:

SCIENTIFIC NAME AND VARIETY:

COMMON NAME:

NOTES ON CARE:

NOTES ON LOCATION:

SCIENTIFIC NAME AND VARIETY:

COMMON NAME:

NOTES ON CARE:

NOTES ON LOCATION:

SCIENTIFIC NAME AND VARIETY:

COMMON NAME:

NOTES ON CARE:

NOTES ON LOCATION:

SCIENTIFIC NAME AND VARIETY:

COMMON NAME:

NOTES ON CARE:

NOTES ON LOCATION:

SCIENTIFIC NAME AND VARIETY:

COMMON NAME:

NOTES ON CARE:

NOTES ON LOCATION:

SCIENTIFIC NAME AND VARIETY:

COMMON NAME:

NOTES ON CARE:

NOTES ON LOCATION:

SCIENTIFIC NAME AND VARIETY:

COMMON NAME:

NOTES ON CARE:

NOTES ON LOCATION:

If we plant in autumn, then we spend winter nurturing the garden's greatest gift: hope.

CHRISTIE PURIFOY

Home in Bloom

CHRISTIE'S

Garden Diary

When I first began to garden, I followed the siren call of the garden centers each spring, spending those glorious first warm days shopping rather than gardening. This meant that weeds gained ground in my garden that I struggled all summer to reclaim, while my newly planted perennials, shrubs, and trees required additional watering all through the hot and dry months. Slowly, I have shifted toward a much more sustainable rhythm. This spring, I planted annuals for my cut flower garden, but otherwise I restrained myself in the garden centers in order to spend more time weeding. Now that it is fall, I have scoured sale racks and assessed the gaps and failures in my garden. In September, October, and even November, my soil is still warm, the sun is gentle, and rainfall is much more predictable. So far this autumn, I have planted evergreen inkberry shrubs and two white oak trees. I also pulled my beautiful burgundy coral bells (heuchera) from their pots and planted them along a shady walkway. The weather has turned unseasonably warm here at the end of October. Perhaps one more visit to the garden center?

PART FOUR

GATHER & CELEBRATE

The word *gather* has two equally important meanings in my garden life: it means *to gather the harvest*, as I do all summer long when I cut flowers or gather up seeds, and it also means *to gather with others in the midst of the garden's beauty*. A meaningful garden party is perhaps my favorite garden harvest.

We traditionally associate harvest with autumn. It is, in our imaginations, the end of the garden year. But gathering, harvesting, and celebrating happen in my garden year-round. Even in winter, I prepare for Christmas by "bringing in the greens," gathering winterberry, holly, and pine in order to bring the evergreen promise of the natural world into the heart of my winter home. But the garden doesn't only help us celebrate the days and moments we already celebrate. The garden gives us *more* that is worthy of celebration. The daffodils help me celebrate Easter, and the winterberry enhances my celebration of Christmas, but thanks to my garden, I now also celebrate the first flush of roses, the first bouquet of dahlias, and the glory of sweet pea perfume.

CELEBRATIONS FOR
Four Seasons

———————

Here are ideas for the celebratory "more" a garden can give.
Of course, you will also find most of us gathered in our gardens on
official calendar holidays, like Father's Day or the Fourth of July.

A LILAC CELEBRATION OR A PEONY PARTY

Special once-a-year flowers deserve our time and attention. Don't let lilac or peony
season pass you by without pausing to appreciate these singular blooms with a flower-
themed picnic or tea party.

STRAWBERRY PARTY

Whether you grow your own or pick them up at a farm stand (I love to use alpine straw-
berries grown from seed in my flower pots), what could be better than a garden party in
honor of this delicious fruit?

RETURN OF THE ROSES

The first flush of roses in late spring or early summer is a perfect excuse to invite people
to gather in your garden while it looks its best.

MIDSUMMER EVE (SUMMER SOLSTICE)

To this day, my favorite garden party was one I hosted on Midsummer Eve for families with young children. We gathered flowers and made flower crowns for everyone. When the circle of the year brings us to the longest day, it is good to pause, to notice all that the garden has given, and to celebrate the gifts of light and life.

FIREFLY CATCH-AND-RELEASE

Each year in my garden, the fireflies and the white oriental lilies make their appearance about the same time. Celebrate both these bright lights with a collection of mason jars, some children, and any garden fairies who happen to join in.

MEMORIAL TREE PLANTING

Fall is the best time to plant a tree, and memorial trees are a wonderful tradition. We can honor loved ones who have died, but we can also plant trees to remember a birth or adoption, a move to a new home, a graduation, or other significant event.

HOLIDAY WREATH PARTY

If you live near a natural area or have a large garden, you can invite guests to gather not only greens but dried grasses, seedheads, and flowers for their holiday wreaths. Sip cider or mulled wine while you work.

My Garden
GATHERINGS

GATHERING:
THEME OR INSPIRATION:
FLOWERS:
MENU:
A SPECIAL MEMORY:

GATHERING:

THEME OR INSPIRATION:

FLOWERS:

MENU:

A SPECIAL MEMORY:

GATHERING:

THEME OR INSPIRATION:

FLOWERS:

MENU:

A SPECIAL MEMORY:

GATHERING:

THEME OR INSPIRATION:

FLOWERS:

MENU:

A SPECIAL MEMORY:

GATHERING:

THEME OR INSPIRATION:

FLOWERS:

MENU:

A SPECIAL MEMORY:

GATHERING:

THEME OR INSPIRATION:

FLOWERS:

MENU:

A SPECIAL MEMORY:

GATHERING:

THEME OR INSPIRATION:

FLOWERS:

MENU:

A SPECIAL MEMORY:

GATHERING:

THEME OR INSPIRATION:

FLOWERS:

MENU:

A SPECIAL MEMORY:

GATHERING:

THEME OR INSPIRATION:

FLOWERS:

MENU:

A SPECIAL MEMORY:

GATHERING:

THEME OR INSPIRATION:

FLOWERS:

MENU:

A SPECIAL MEMORY:

My Flowers:
A LOOK BACK

What did you love this year
and why? What do you want
to plant again next year?

YEAR:

MY FLOWERS

YEAR:

YEAR:

MY FLOWERS

YEAR:

YEAR:

MY FLOWERS

YEAR:

YEAR:

MY FLOWERS

YEAR:

MY FLOWERS

YEAR:

MY FLOWERS

YEAR:

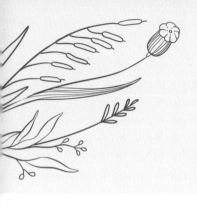

My Seeds
TO SAVE

DATE GATHERED	PLANT NAME

Just about any flower seeds can be saved, but seeds saved from hybrid varieties will not look like their parent plants. Seeds saved from heirloom, open-pollinated plants should closely resemble their parent. When gathering, look for flowers that have lost their petals or whose petals have turned brown. On a sunny day, after the dew has dried, snip the flowerheads into a bowl or tray. Spread the ripe seeds out to dry on parchment paper, waxed paper, or paper plates. I avoid paper towels, which might encourage damp seeds to germinate. Allow to dry for about a week before storing seeds, minus any husks or pods, in sealed paper envelopes.

DATE GATHERED	PLANT NAME

SEEDS TO SAVE

DATE GATHERED	PLANT NAME

SEEDS TO SAVE

DATE GATHERED	PLANT NAME

SEEDS TO SAVE

DATE GATHERED	PLANT NAME

SEEDS TO SAVE

DATE GATHERED	PLANT NAME

SEEDS TO SAVE

DATE GATHERED	PLANT NAME

SEEDS TO SAVE

DATE GATHERED	PLANT NAME

My Plants
TO DIVIDE

DATE DIVIDED	PLANT NAME

Dividing perennials is a great way to create more plants for our gardens. It also helps plants to stay vigorous and healthy. Feel free to divide any plant that has enough roots to support multiple pieces, but you will know a plant needs dividing if it has died out in its center, is flowering less, or seems to have grown too large. Dividing is usually best accomplished in spring or fall. Delicate plants can be lifted and their roots gently teased apart. Robust plants, like nepeta and hosta, can be sliced with a sharp knife or spade.

DATE DIVIDED	PLANT NAME

PLANTS TO DIVIDE

DATE DIVIDED	PLANT NAME

PLANTS TO DIVIDE

DATE DIVIDED	PLANT NAME

PLANTS TO DIVIDE

DATE DIVIDED	PLANT NAME

PLANTS TO DIVIDE

DATE DIVIDED	PLANT NAME

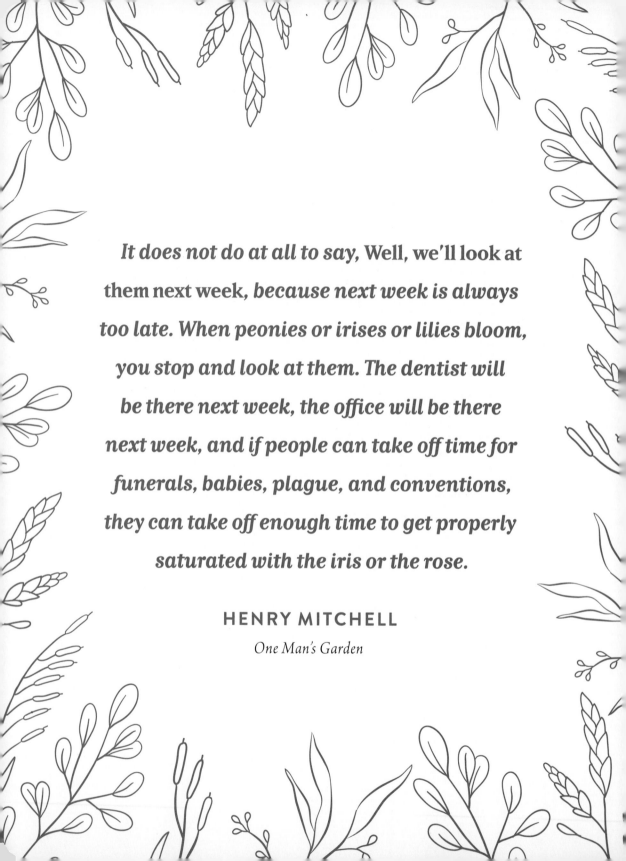

It does not do at all to say, Well, we'll look at them next week, because next week is always too late. When peonies or irises or lilies bloom, you stop and look at them. The dentist will be there next week, the office will be there next week, and if people can take off time for funerals, babies, plague, and conventions, they can take off enough time to get properly saturated with the iris or the rose.

HENRY MITCHELL

One Man's Garden

Garden Diary

This year my top seed-saving priority is the purple chilies from a friend in Texas. They proved to be delicious, prolific, and ornamental. I even used branches cut from my enormous plants in autumn bouquets. This year was quite dry, and my flower garden is somehow looking both overgrown and dried out. It is not a pretty sight, but as I dropped ripe chilies into a bowl, I considered how to turn my disappointment into hope. Laying my saved chili seeds aside, I began cutting back the garden bits browned by drought and let myself imagine how I might improve the garden next year. Failure can be good compost, but I must turn the failures over in my mind like I turn my compost pile with a garden fork. While I worked and while I thought, my frustrations and my disappointments gradually transformed themselves into new ideas and new dreams, and I felt—beneath my feet and in my heart—another turn in the circle of my flower garden life.

ABOUT THE AUTHOR

CHRISTIE PURIFOY is a writer and gardener who loves to grow flowers and community. She is the author of *Garden Maker: Growing a Life of Beauty and Wonder with Flowers*, *A Home in Bloom: Four Enchanted Seasons with Flowers*, and *Seedtime and Harvest: How Gardens Grow Roots, Connection, Wholeness, and Hope*.

Christie earned a PhD in English literature from the University of Chicago but eventually traded the classroom for an old Pennsylvania farmhouse called Maplehurst, where, along with her husband and four children, she welcomes frequent guests to the Maplehurst Black Barn.

CHRISTIEPURIFOY.COM | BLACKBARNGARDENCLUB.COM